Growing up in
ANCIENT GREECE

Philippa Stewart

B.T. Batsford Ltd *London*

© Philippa Stewart 1980
First published 1980

ISBN 0 7134 3376 0

Printed by The Garden City Press Ltd
Letchworth, Herts
for the Publishers B T Batsford Limited
4 Fitzhardinge Street, London W1H 0AH

Frontispiece: **"The blond youth"**

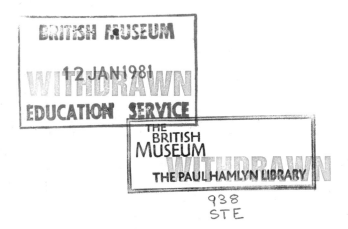

Acknowledgment

The Author and Publishers thank the following for
their kind permission to reproduce copyright
illustrations: BBC Hulton Picture Library for figs 8,
14, 15, 20, 25, 27, 30, 40, 46, 53, 55, 58; The
Trustees of the British Museum for figs 7, 21, 49,
52; Chartwell Illustrators for fig 2; Mary Evans
Picture Library for fig 50; Greek Tourist Office for
figs 9, 10, 11, 24, 26, 28, 29, 32, 35, 36, 37, 48; Pat
Hodgson Picture Research Agency for figs 3, 6, 38;
A.F.Kersting for figs 12, 51; Mansell Collection for
figs 4, 5, 13, 17, 23, 34, 39, 41, 42, 43, 44, 47, 54,
56, 57; Museum of Fine Arts, Boston for fig 22;
Victoria and Albert Museum for figs 16, 18, 19, 31,
33. Thanks also are expressed to Pat Hodgson for
the picture research.

Contents

The Illustrations

1 The Cradle of Western Civilization

For centuries men seeking out the truth about life, its meaning and man's worth have turned their attention towards a small and mountainous country, and a civilization that flourished for a few hundred years in the fifth and fourth centuries BC.

The stern Romans, with their great ideas of Empire and discipline, sent their sons to study in Greece, and based their art on Greek examples. The tremendous flowering of the Renaissance in Europe owed much of its inspiration to the rediscovery of Greek thought.

The Ancient Greeks have left us something to remember them by, and admire them for, in almost every field. Western philosophy has its origins in the doctrines of Greek thinkers such as Plato and Socrates. Our theatrical tradition is based on the Greek examples of Aeschylus, Euripides, Sophocles (tragedy), and Aristophanes (comedy). The experiments of Pythagoras, Archimedes and Euclid laid the foundations for our thinking on mathematics, physics and geometry. The Greek, Hippocrates was the first scientific doctor, observing and meticulously recording the symptoms of his patients. Herodotus is known as "the father of

1   Hermes, by the Athenian sculptor Praxiteles. The statue seems to express the Greeks' belief in the value of individual personality.

history", with his attempt at an accurate and verified historical record. The list of what the Western world owes to the Greeks is endless, for in almost every branch of art and science we trace our origins back to them, and start from them when thinking afresh.

But perhaps the most enduring, and certainly the most important legacy left to us by the Greeks is something that we take so much for granted that it is hard to realize the extent to which it set the Greeks apart from the rest of the world. The Greeks were the first civilization to propound (and, to some extent, to put into practice) a belief in the value of individual man, not respecting someone more because he is rich and powerful, but considering rich and poor, weak and strong alike as equals before the law. The great Athenian statesman Pericles declared: "Each single one of our citizens, in every aspect of life, is able to show himself the rightful lord and owner of his own person." This belief is at the core of the Greeks' social and political system called democracy (in Greek = "rule by the people"), and is a fundamental cornerstone of our own traditions.

The main purpose of education in Ancient Greece was to instil in the young Greek a high sense of his own worth as an individual, and to encourage him always to strive for his own personal standards of excellence. This meant that in adult life, too, the Greeks had very high expectations of themselves. They were never content to be just one of a crowd, but were trained always to push themselves to the limits of their own expertise, whether as craftsmen or soldiers, traders or philosophers.

The high personal expectations drilled into them in childhood probably account for much of what we today so admire about the Greeks.

In this book we shall be looking at what it was like to grow up in Ancient Greece, trying to understand how a small and in many ways rather backward country was able to contribute so much to our understanding of civilization, and seeing how young Greeks prepared themselves to play a full part in the running of their state.

The picture of growing up is, of necessity, slightly hazy, since the Greeks themselves were not at all concerned to chronicle their childhood. They believed that it was only grown man, with his faculties fully developed, and displaying the all-round excellence (arete) which they so admired, who was worthy of serious attention. Childhood and growing up were seen merely as necessary, if slightly tedious, preparations for this.

We shall be looking mainly at Athens, partly because we know more about Athens, and partly because Athens had an important influence on the rest of Greece. The information on which this book is based comes in many forms: clues found in literature and drama, details from sculpture, paintings on pottery, the remains of buildings both large and small, and the tools that the Greeks once used.

2 Historical Background

The land and its people

The first things that strike any visitor to Greece in summer are the sunshine, and the barrenness of the landscape. It is a rocky, often mountainous country, with small deep valleys surrounded by hard limestone hills, and brightly lit under a clear blue sky. There is almost no rain in the middle of summer, and very few rivers have water in them all the year round. The craggy coast is deeply indented by the sea; indeed the sea is never very far away in Greece. To the south, the pattern of the landscape is continued by strings of hundreds of small rocky islands, not all of which are inhabited.

Greece is not a rich country. The soil on even the lower slopes of the hills is generally too poor for cultivation, and is used for

2 Greece

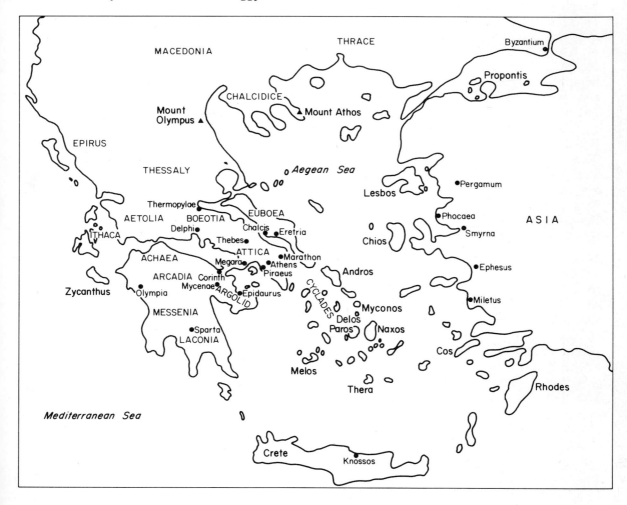

grazing sheep and goats. This leaves just the narrow strips of valley as cultivatable land, and it was along these that the characteristic Greek city-states developed, small self-contained communities, isolated from one another by the harsh mountains, and needing to be totally self-reliant.

Most states had their strip of fertile plain, of hillside pasture, of forested mountain slope and barren mountain top, and usually access to the sea as well. Although Greece

3 A view from the temple of Delphi. The land is barren except for the narrow valleys.

is remembered for the glory of its town life, it is important to realize that the men who took part in this town life were basically farmers, and that the town was no more in most cases than a market centre such as the English market towns, relying for its life on the comings and goings of a farming community.

8

Who were the Greeks?

The origin of the Greek people is lost in the mists of time. But we do know that in about 2000 BC wandering tribes from Russia in the north filtered down into Greece, settling and mixing with the people there. From this mixture the Greek language developed.

The Mycenaean civilization

From about 1600 to 1200 BC a great Bronze Age civilization flourished in Greece. It is called Mycenaean, after the citadel of Mycenae where its remains were first uncovered. Although the history of the Mycenaean era is muddled up with legend, for the Greeks loved to make up stories about their great ancestors, we do know that in the Mycenaean age Greece was ruled by kings who built great palaces surrounded by thick stone walls, and ate off rich gold plate. Complicated accounts seem to have been kept by court officials, and trading ships from Greece travelled all over the eastern Mediterranean.

The siege of Troy

In about 1200 BC the Mycenaean kings collected together a great army, set sail across the Aegean Sea and laid siege to the city of Troy on the north-west coast of present-day Turkey. This siege forms the basis of the Greek poet Homer's immense narrative poem, the *Iliad*. For centuries it was believed that Homer had invented the story, until a German archaeologist

4   Gold funeral mask of 1560 BC, found at the citadel of Mycenae.

Heinrich Schliemann, by dint of careful research and excavations, uncovered the site of the ancient city of Troy, which had indeed been destroyed by war in the thirteenth century BC.

In the *Iliad* Homer describes how the quarrelsome Greek warriors, after ten years of siege, finally gained access to the city by building a wooden horse, hiding a band of picked men inside it, and then pretending to sail away. The Trojans, duped, took the horse into the city. At night the Greek soldiers inside the horse climbed out and opened the city gates to the rest of their army, who swiftly overwhelmed the Trojans. Troy was sacked.

The Dark Ages
But the siege of Troy marked the end of the

5 Mycenaean wall painting of a two-wheeled chariot.

glory of the Mycenaean age. During the next 200 years, warlike tribes from the north invaded the Mediterranean, cutting off trade routes and plundering palaces as they went. The Mycenaean kings could no longer keep up their luxurious way of life, and started fighting amongst themselves. Soon even the art of writing had been lost, and Greece descended into the Dark Ages, so

6 Mycenaean palace at Tyrins.

called because very little is known about the period.

The Archaic period
Slowly Greece came out of the Dark Ages, and culture and civilization revived. It was in about 850 BC, for example, that Homer

7 A scene from the Trojan war depicted on an *amphora* of 540-530 BC. Achilles slays Penthesilea, the Queen of the Amazons.

people a share in the land. The word "tyrant" did not have the same pejorative meaning for the Greeks as it has for us today, and simply meant "strong ruler". In other states, magistrates were appointed to govern and set up oligarchies (or "rule by a few").

In 594 BC Solon was appointed chief magistrate of Athens, and began the move towards democracy. He allowed all citizens to vote in the Assembly, and set up juries to try law cases. Over the next century the Assembly became the most powerful part of the government, giving the whole of the citizen body a say in the running of the state. All citizens were eligible for government posts, which were decided by election.

Everywhere laws were being codified, and people's rights and responsibilities laid down. At the same time the arts and sciences began to flourish.

Warring city-states

On and off throughout this period the cities of mainland Greece were at war with one another, forming alliances and leagues, fighting quick skirmishes and then retiring, organizing raiding parties each summer to plunder their enemy's land and crops. Some of these wars seem very petty in origin, a matter of honour or an assumed slight. Others were more serious, concerning perhaps a state's right to trade or access to the sea.

Gradually, over the centuries, two states became predominant: the mainland state of Sparta holding sway over a large part of the Peloponnese, and the maritime state of Athens whose strength lay in her navy and control of the sea.

The Persian wars

The only time the Greek cities set aside their interminable internal squabbles was to

wrote his two epic poems, the *Iliad* and the *Odyssey*. City-states began to form as people moved from their villages to live around the central fort or *polis*.

As the population grew, different states evolved different forms of government. In some, the traditional aristocracy, the kings and princes left over from the Mycenaean age, were overthrown by strong men, known as tyrants, who promised the

8 A Greek warrior. ➤

12

Greek tragedians: 9 Euripides; 10 Sophocles;
11 Aeschylus

present a common front against the threat
of outside invasion. In 480 BC Xerxes,
ruler of the great Persian Empire, sent a
huge army to invade Greece. His intention
was to punish Athens for fostering a revolt
in a Persian-ruled city.

Their differences set aside, the Greek
states combined. Three hundred Spartans
held the mountain pass at Thermopylae
for two days against the entire Persian
army, to enable the Athenians to evacuate
their city. In the bay of Salamis, the largely
Athenian navy put rout to the Persian fleet.

The Classical age
The next fifty years saw the true flowering
of Greek civilization, particularly in Athens,
in a period known as the Classical age. This
was the time when Aeschylus, Sophocles
and Euripides wrote their great tragedies;
when Socrates and Plato were teaching men
new ways to think; when the Parthenon was

being built, and the greatest sculpture
carved. It was an age of hope and great
ideals, which has seldom if ever been equalled.
It is also the period with which the rest of
this book is mainly concerned.

The Athenian Empire, the Peloponnesian War, and Alexander the Great
Athens became more powerful. She formed
a league of friendly states, each of whom
had to pay tribute every year for the upkeep
of her navy, in return for protection. States
who tried to withdraw from the Athenian
League were punished.

Sparta was quick to come to the rescue
of such states, and in 431 BC war broke out
again between Athens and Sparta. However,
because Sparta was mainly strong on land
and Athens was mainly a sea power, they
failed to get properly to grips with one
another, and the war dragged on for year
after year, dangerously weakening both
parties.

Finally Sparta, with help from Persia,
blocked the sea-routes to Athens, thus

14

12 Part of the Erechtheum, built on the Acropolis next to the Parthenon in Athens — a fine example of Classical Greek sculpture.

cutting off her corn supply, and Athens was forced to surrender. But although Sparta was the victor, she was now too weak to be able to rule over the whole of Greece.

Sporadic fighting continued until 350 BC, when Greece was conquered by Philip of Macedon, which is part of modern Yugoslavia. Philip's son Alexander went on to conquer the greatest Empire the world had seen.

The decline of Greece
At his death, however, Alexander the Great

13 Ancient Greece has fascinated artists and thinkers for centuries. Some of the pictures in this book, like this one of a ship of the Greek navy, show nineteenth-century interpretations of Greek life. It is interesting to notice that these do not really capture the greatness of Greek civilization, even though man has made such progress.

left no strong successor, and as his generals fought amongst themselves his Empire disintegrated. Meanwhile, in the west, a new power was growing up around the Italian city of Rome, whose influence gradually spread all over the Mediterranean. By 146 BC Greece was part of the Roman Empire.

3 A Greek Home

We are used to thinking of the Ancient Greeks as civilized; but if we are really to understand what it was like to grow up and live in Ancient Greece we shall have to strip away a whole layer of preconceptions about what "to be civilized" means.

For the Greeks, civilization was not measured in terms of material possessions or comforts, for they had very few of those. Most of the things we take for granted were completely unknown in Greece. It is easy to imagine life, perhaps, without television or cars; but we must also imagine houses without drains or running water, where the only light at night came from oil torches, and the only heat in winter from a pot of warm ashes; rooms with scarcely any furniture, beds without any springs or sheets, clothes without any buttons or zips. We must imagine what it was like to tell the time without a watch, or to discuss politics without a newspaper. On the material level, the Greeks' way of life was utterly different from our own.

The house
The first thing to remember is that the climate in Greece allowed houses to be built much more simply than ours. Greek men spent most of their time out of doors; for them the house was just a place to eat and sleep. The women spent most of their time at home, but because of the warm climate preferred to be in the open air rather than under cover.

Greek houses were built to suit this way of life. They consisted of a series of rooms leading off a central courtyard. The rooms provided cool and shade away from the glare of the sun, and shelter at night, but the courtyard, often with a colonnade around it, and the hall leading off it were the focal points of domestic life. Other rooms might include an anteroom or porter's lodge, several bedrooms, a dining room and another smaller living-room, a kitchen and store-room, a room for the use of household slaves, and even a bathroom.

The houses were built of mud bricks, often rising straight from the ground, without any foundations. A narrow entrance fronted on to the street, with the rest of the house hidden behind its walls. Sometimes the walls were so soft that burglars could simply dig their way in (burglars in Greece were known as "wall-breakers"). The walls inside were decorated with painted plaster, and the floors paved with mosaics. At night the courtyard was lit by lamps set in niches in the wall. There were no fireplaces, and in winter charcoal braziers provided the only warmth (and, incidentally, a lot of smoke).

Home life
The Greek writer Xenophon, in his book *Oeconomicus* (Economics), described the different roles of men and women in Greek society. The men spent most of their time away from the house, rising at dawn, working in the morning on the farm or in the workshop, doing the shopping (with a slave to carry the purchases back to the house), and carrying out civic duties as a juryman or council member. They spent the after-

14   Inside a home in Athens. This is a reconstruction.

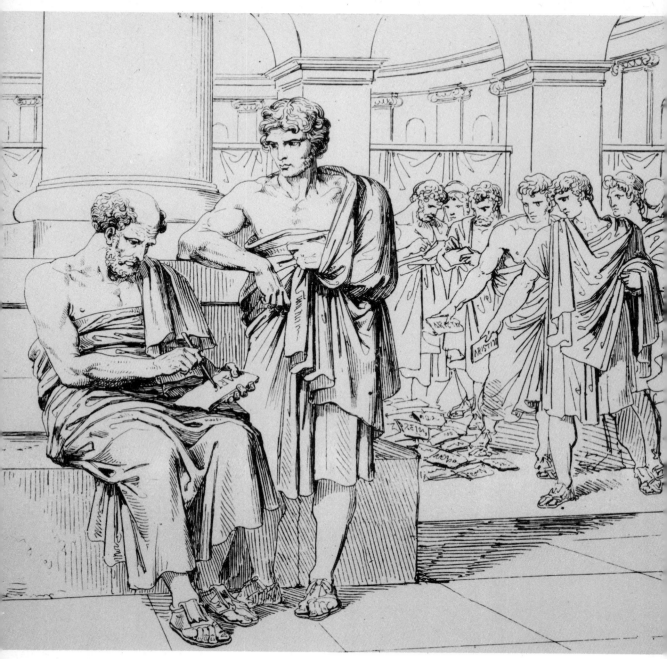

15 An artist's impression of Greek democracy. Athenian citizens voted to decide whether someone should be exiled or not. Here a vote is being taken about Aristides, who is writing his name for a stranger who wants him banished. The voting was done by placing the voting card on either the left- or the right-hand pile.

noon at the theatre or the gymnasium, or just talking with friends in the market place (the agora), and they only returned home in the evening to eat. Even meal-times were often strictly segregated affairs, with all-male dinner parties being the norm

rather than the exception.

The wife meanwhile was in charge of organizing the household work. This included overseeing the weaving, looking after the stores of wine and corn, supervising the slaves and teaching new slaves their duties, caring for the sick and looking after the children. Greek women seldom set foot out of doors, except for an occasional visit to friends or for a religious festival, but within the home their authority was all-embracing.

Furniture

Furniture in a Greek house was kept to a minimum. There were chests to store blankets in, but no cupboards or wardrobes. Most things were hung from nails in the wall.

The most important piece of furniture in the house was the high couch on which the men reclined at mealtimes, and which doubled up at night as a bed. Food was served on low rectangular tables, which often had only three legs. The tables were low enough so that they could be pushed under the couches when the meal was finished. Women did not eat lying on couches, but instead sat on small stools or chairs.

Chairs came in a variety of shapes and sizes, ranging from large throne-like seats of honour, with carved feet and elegant arms and back, to the more homely chairs used by women while weaving or spinning. There were also small footstools.

Pots

Apart from wooden furniture, and a few bronze boxes and trinkets, almost all household goods, from lamps and cooking pots to tiles and toys, were made of clay. Although pottery breaks easily, it is virtually indestructible, and the remains of Greek pottery, beautifully decorated with scenes of everyday life and mythological tales, are one of

17 A parting scene from a tomb of the fifth century BC. The lady sitting is the dead woman, Hegeso. She is shown choosing a necklace out of her jewel box which is held by her maid. The necklace was probably painted on the tombstone, and does not show now. The tomb is interesting for the idea it gives of a Greek chair, and of Greek costumes and hairstyles.

the best records we have of life in Ancient Greece.

The pots came in many different shapes and sizes, depending on their intended use, and ranged from wine coolers and drinking bowls to scent bottles and delicate dishes.

Athenian pots, with their distinctive black glaze decoration, were admired all over the ancient world, and formed an important part of Athenian exports.

18 A drinking goblet in the shape of a boar's head, 460 BC.

▼

Clothes

It was the job of the women to make all the clothes needed by the household. A whole sheep's fleece would be bought in the market, and dyed, spun and woven at home as required.

There were no changing fashions in Greek clothes. Men and women, young and old, wore basically the same: a large rectangular piece of cloth, folded over and attached at the shoulders and then tied around the waist to form a tunic. This was known as a *chiton* (see picture 12). It was worn short, to the knee, by children and young men; and ankle-length by women and older men, and for all ceremonial occasions. For wear outdoors, and to keep warm in the winter, another rectangular piece of cloth was used as a mantle. The Greeks did not bother with nightclothes, or even with underwear,

19 A Greek vase of about 400 BC.

23

20 A Greek *krater,* with a design of a chariot. The *krater* was used for mixing wine with water.

though occasionally a woman might wear a narrow strip of cloth as a brassière.

Although they all dressed in basically the same way, the Greeks were able to add individuality in the colours of their tunics, which were dyed with a selection of vegetable dyes to bright orange, yellow, green or blue, or decorated with borders or patterned all over. Sometimes they were even pleated.

Hairstyles were very varied. By the fifth century BC most men wore their hair cropped short, but women (apart from slaves) kept their hair long, and draped and plaited it around their heads, keeping it in place perhaps with a ribbon or scarf or a tiara-like headband. Women also wore rings, bracelets and necklaces, and sometimes earrings as well. Most jewellery was made of gold, and inset with coral and agate and other semi-precious stones.

Footwear was simple and kept to a minimum. Many Greeks went barefoot both indoors and out. The most common form of footwear was sandals, tied with thongs up the leg. In winter and when travelling, men often wore soft leather boots. And because height was considered an attribute, some women put cork soles on their shoes to make them appear taller.

Although Greek men liked to be bronzed and suntanned, they admired women with pale white skin. For this reason many women used white lead to paint their faces. They also sometimes put soot around their eyes, and tinted their cheeks with mulberry juice.

Washing arrangements

Very few houses had their own water supply. The central courtyard of the house might contain a pool to collect rainwater, but generally the water was fetched from a

21 Part of the decoration of a Greek vase, showing costume. The woman on the left has an embroidered cap, a necklace, a bracelet, a *chiton* and a mantle. She is holding out a mirror. Next stands a youth wearing a mantle and sandals. On the right is a woman with her hair tied in a knot, an embroidered open cap, necklace, and a *chiton* with a double stripe down the side.

25

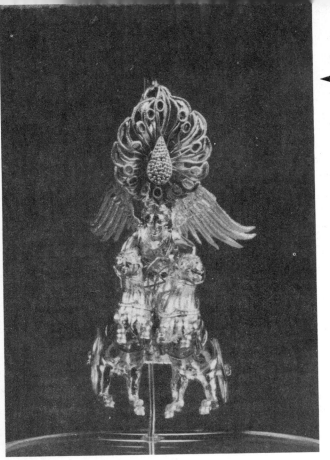

◄ 22 A gold earring, in the shape of a Greek chariot, of the fourth century BC.

fountain in the street, by women (usually slaves) who carried the heavy water-pots on their heads.

The Greeks liked to take care of their bodies, and to keep clean and well groomed. Many houses had a separate bathroom, with a large earthenware or bronze bath, which was filled with water carried from the fountain. There were plenty of sponges, but no soap. Instead, the Greeks used oil, or a special sort of mud, fuller's earth, which they rubbed all over their bodies and then scraped off with a square-ended instrument called a strigil.

Athens had official refuse collectors; but in general all rubbish was thrown into the street, down the middle of which ran an open drain which also served as a sewer.

23 Women washing at a fountain, under a colonnade. The picture is taken from a vase of about 520 BC.
▼

24 Women carrying water-pots on their shoulders. A sculpture from the Acropolis.

Meals

On the whole, the Greeks ate very simply. Breakfast usually consisted of bread dipped in diluted wine. Lunch might be bread again, with some goat's-milk cheese or olives and figs. The only hot meal of the day was in the evening. It was usually served as two courses: first fish with perhaps vegetables, followed by cheese, cakes and fruit. Meat was seldom eaten, being reserved for festivals and other special occasions.

Wine was the main drink, but the Greeks thought it dissolute to drink it neat. Instead, they mixed it with water in a special pot called a *krater* before drinking it in carefully controlled quantities.

In the evening, rather than eating with their wives, Greek men often went to all-male dinner and drinking parties (called symposiums in Greek). There, after they had

27

eaten, they discussed politics and philosophical matters, took turns to compose songs and poems, made up riddles and games, or were entertained by dancing girls and flute players.

Household slaves

Several times in this chapter we have referred to slaves. Although the Ancient Greeks considered themselves the great protectors of individual liberty, this did not extend to foreigners, to women or to slaves, of whom there were many thousands in Athens alone during the Classical period.

Slavery was one of the hazards of life at the time. Anyone could become a slave — by being captured in war, for example, or kidnapped by pirates at sea. An established citizen thus enslaved could be redeemed by his family or friends if they could collect the necessary ransom. But in many cases this was not possible. Thousands of other people were born into slavery.

Most slaves were well treated. The men were usually employed on the land, or as craftsmen in workshops. The women helped with the housework, and looked after the children. Household slaves were treated as part of the family; and many tombstone inscriptions bear witness to the feelings of affection which existed between them and their masters.

25 A Greek family meal, redrawn from a frieze sculpture. It was more usual for men to dine separately from the women.

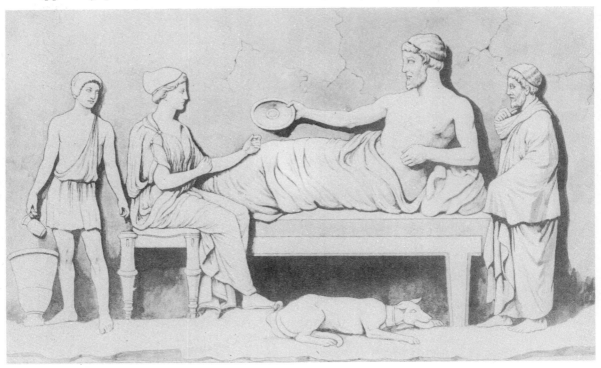

4 The Birth of a Child

Survival of the fittest

In his play *Oedipus Rex*, Sophocles describes how when the baby Oedipus was only a few hours old, his father ordered him to be placed on a bare mountainside and left there to die. And, indeed, this is what would have happened had not a shepherd taken pity on the child and rescued him.

Today this story fills us with horror, but it was not an uncommon occurrence in Ancient Greece, even in the Classical period. The soil in Greece was not particularly fertile; too many mouths to feed could mean starvation for all. Children were expensive to rear, especially girls, for whom a dowry had to be provided. There was no spare capacity to look after crippled, deformed or sickly children. So the Greeks, knowing nothing about birth control, evolved their own system for keeping a check on the population, making sure that only the fit survived, and that there was enough food for everyone.

For the first ten days after a child was born, its father had the right to decide whether or not it was going to live. If he decided against it, the child was packed into a cradle or pot and left exposed in a public place. It was hoped that some other citizen, perhaps with more resources or fewer children of his own, would find the child and accept it into his household.

The naming ceremony

If the father decided to keep the child, religious rites were carried out on the fifth day after birth; and on the tenth day, in a solemn naming ceremony, the child was officially presented to the household and accepted into its midst. From then on there could be no question of renouncing it; the child was now part of the household, to be loved and cared for in sickness and in health; and, at least to begin with, spoilt too, for the Ancient Greeks were very fond of children.

The role of the mother

For the first six years of life the child stayed at home, under the mother's direct supervision. It was her task to organize a life that would be "free of sorrow, fear and pain" during the first three years, and "full of sports and amusements" in the next three.

During these early years the mother's influence was all important, and fathers did not interfere in the upbringing of their children. Many records show, however, that fathers were very fond of their children, playing with them and buying them presents whenever the opportunity arose. A character in Greek comedy, for example, says to his son: "The first money I ever earned as a juryman I spent on a toy chariot for you."

Nurseries and nannies

Most Greek houses, even those belonging to the very rich, did not have a separate nursery. The young children spent most of their time playing in the courtyard, or in the women's quarters.

There was usually at least one nurse, either a slave or a free woman, in charge of them. Spartan women were said to be best

26 Family scene from a tombstone.

▲
27 Pictures of children at play, taken from Greek vases.

28 Clay models of about the seventh century BC. ►

for this, as they were both firm and sensible. And, of course, there were all the other members of the household too, to talk to and watch and play with, so that a Greek child's early years, in the safety of the household courtyard, were usually very jolly.

Nursery furniture
Many remains have been found of furniture designed specifically for children — small cots, feeding bottles, a form of high chair on a solid-looking rocking base.

Toys and games
Greek toys were not very different from the toys we know today. For the very young there were rattles, made out of wood or, more often, pottery, and filled with small stones. Or there were toy chariots, two-wheeled carts, to pull about, or a hobby-horse built out of a simple wheel attached to a long pole.

Older children also had toy chariots, larger ones, in which they could sit and be pulled along by dogs or goats, or by another child. "Chariot-racing" was a popular game.

Small toys included models of chariots, and of horses, birds and other animals made

31

out of clay or wood. Girls had dolls, made of various materials. Many Greek girls, who were married at the age of fourteen or fifteen, played with dolls until their wedding day.

From paintings on pottery and sculpture, we can see that the Ancient Greeks enjoyed many of the games children still play today. There are pictures of them bowling hoops (which were made of iron, and often had bells and rings attached to produce a tinkling sound as the hoop rolled), or playing with a yo-yo or a whipping-top; other scenes show swings and seesaws being used, or games of piggy-back or ball games. Knucklebones (or jacks) were a popular pastime, and were played by women as well as children.

The Greeks also had board games, though we do not know exactly what they consisted of — probably a form of draughts.

Pets
Most Greek households kept some livestock, both to provide food and to serve as pets. Tortoises, hares and dogs seem to have been the most popular pets; cats, on the other hand and rather surprisingly, were almost unknown. Poultry and ornamental birds were also common.

The early years
For the first six years of life, then, the Greek child was kept cosseted and well amused within the safe confines of the women's quarters in the home.

But, after their sixth birthday, boys and girls were separated from one another, and the serious business of life began. Girls remained at home with their mothers, learning how to run a household and preparing themselves for marriage (see pages 42-50), while boys were sent off to school to learn to be men.

29 Girl with a pet rabbit.

5 An Athenian Youth

In this chapter we shall be looking at what it was like to be a typical young boy growing up in Athens in the Classical period. Every city-state in Greece had its different customs, but many of the things described here would have been the same in most other Greek cities.

School

Boys went to school from the age of six until about fifteen. Classes were held in the morning only, and the boy would go off soon after dawn, accompanied by a special slave, often elderly, called a pedagogue (in Greek = "boy-leader"). His job was to keep the boy out of trouble, and perhaps help the schoolmaster to maintain order in the classroom.

Schools were not run by the state, but had to be financed out of the fees paid by parents. Most schools had a special building, divided up into separate classrooms, but sometimes classes were held in the open air, in the streets, if that was all the schoolmaster could afford.

At school, a boy learned to read and write, to count, to play the lyre, and to sing, dance and recite poetry.

Reading and writing

The first thing was to learn how to read and write. The boy had to learn the Greek alphabet and practise forming the letters. Papyrus (paper) was expensive and difficult to obtain, and so was generally reserved for important documents only.

At school, writing was done on wax-coated tablets, with a sharp instrument known as a stylus. The tablets were made of wood, with a central panel of wax protected by a raised edge. When an exercise was finished, the wax could be smoothed with the flat end of the stylus and then used again.

For convenience, several tablets were sometimes strung together. The string passed through holes bored in their wooden edges.

Counting

The Ancient Greeks did not have special symbols for their numbers, but used letters of the alphabet as numerals. This meant that doing sums on paper was quite difficult.

30 Boys were taught to write, read and play the lyre.

Instead, the Greeks evolved a system of counting using pebbles (the Greek word "calculus" means "pebble", and has given us many English words, including calculate); or else a special counting-board known as an abacus.

The abacus is a very efficient form of counting, and is still used today in many parts of the world. At its simplest it consists of a board with three wires strung across it. On each wire there are ten beads, which can be moved along the wire as the counting proceeds. The bottom wire represents single units, from one to ten. The beads on the next wire are worth ten units each (10 x 10 = 100); and the beads on the top wire are worth one hundred units each (10 x 100 = 1000). By moving the beads back and forth along the wires, it was possible to do any number of additions and subtractions, and even simple multiplication and division, without difficulty.

One advantage of the abacus system was that it allowed the Greeks to see very clearly (more clearly than we often do)

31 A girl playing the pan-pipes, painted on an *amphora.*

the relationship between numbers, the difference between odd, even and prime numbers, for example. Numbers were not just symbols scratched on a piece of paper, but became solid, three-dimensional objects, which a boy could touch and move, play and experiment with. This may help to explain why the Greeks were so good at abstract mathematical thought, and formulated many of the mathematic and geometric concepts which we still use today.

Music

Music was considered an essential part of every Greek boy's education.

The instrument most commonly used in schools was the lyre, which had seven strings which were plucked to accompany the chanting of poetry. Other instruments included the flute (which probably sounded rather like our modern oboe), and pipes (or pan-pipes) which were traditionally played by shepherds.

Many illustrations of classroom scenes show a music lesson in progress, with the master either listening to a pupil or demonstrating how to play. In many others there are musical instruments hanging on the wall in the background.

Literature, poetry and recitation

The core of Greek education was provided by the works of Homer. His two long epic poems, the *Iliad* (which tells the story of the Trojan War and the siege of Troy), and the *Odyssey* (which describes the adventures of the Greek hero Odysseus on his way home from the war), were studied in minute detail, and great chunks learnt by heart by all Greek schoolboys. The Greeks considered that larger-than-life stories of gods and heroes improved the mind and provided worthy examples to follow in life.

Boys studied the poems for their narrative element and for the way they were written. They learned their history from them, and their geography, and their religion.

34

32 "The blond youth", a famous Greek sculpture of the Archaic period. Notice the hairstyle.

Greek poetry was meant to be heard, not read; reciting Homer's words taught young Greeks the art of rhetoric, or speaking in public, and a proper cadence of speech.

And because the works of Homer were studied by all Greeks, they provided a common experience, and a core of "Greekness", which was shared by all.

Discipline

Once he had started school, a Greek boy was considered to have left the gentle world of women and to be preparing himself to be a man. This meant that his upbringing became suddenly much more strict. One Greek writer described how "as soon as he is able to understand what is being said to him, mother and nurse and father and tutor are vying with one another to improve the child . . . . If he obeys, well and good; if not, he is straightened by threats and blows, like a piece of bent or warped wood."

The slipper seems to have been the favourite form of punishment. Both at school and at home, the Greek boy was not allowed to forget that he was striving for all-round excellence.

Sport

After a morning at school, the Greek schoolboy usually spent his afternoon in the palaestra, or training ground, or in the rather larger gymnasium, testing and improving his physical strength.

The Ancient Greeks greatly prized physical prowess and believed in the "complete" man, one whose mind and whose body were both in top condition. Of course, sport was also very good training for war.

On arrival the boy stripped off his clothes, for the Greeks liked to exercise naked. He then rubbed himself over with olive oil before going on to the exercise ground. Here, on a sandy floor, a trainer taught wrestling, boxing, jumping, and throwing the javelin or discus. In the larger gymnasiums, there were also running tracks and other facilities.

The boys were encouraged to push themselves as far as they could go; there was no holding back or rules of fair play, and all sport in Ancient Greece was extremely competitive.

After several hours of strenuous exercise the boys used a flat-bladed instrument called a strigil to scrape the oil and sand off their bodies before getting dressed.

The Games

Grown men too exercised in the gymnasiums, and took part in the regular sporting competitions, or Games, that were held all over Greece, usually in honour of a god. The most famous of these are the Olympic

Games, held every four years from 776 BC onwards, but there were many others.

People came from all over Greece to watch the Games (the Games, incidentally, had a useful side-effect of making warring city-states put aside their arms, at least temporarily). And it was considered a great honour to participate, though the prizes themselves were very modest — a crown of laurel leaves, perhaps, or a jar of oil.

The most famous and the main event in the Games was the Pentathlon, in which the athlete had to compete in five different sports (thus satisfying the Greeks' desire for *arete*, or excellence in everything). The five events of the Pentathlon were: 1. running (usually one length of the stadium, or roughly 180 metres; the Ancient Olympics did not include a marathon race); 2. discus throwing (the discus was a flat, circular bronze plate, weighing about 2 to 3 kg, which the athlete had to swing in his hand and then throw as far as possible); 3. long jump (in which the athletes jumped from a standing position and often had to hold weights; sometimes they were accompanied by flute players); 4. wrestling (no holds were barred, and a fall on any part of the body counted; three falls brought victory, and even tripping was allowed); and 5. javelin throwing (the Greek javelin, or spear, was about the height of a man, and was thrown with the help of a leather thong about halfway along the shaft, into which the athlete slipped his first two fingers, before launching the javelin with a slight twisting movement).

To win the Pentathlon was considered the highest possible honour for a Greek, and successful athletes were treated as conquering heroes when they returned home to their cities; sometimes a hole was specially dug through the city wall to allow them to enter; others were exempted from tax for the rest of their lives, or allotted a permanent seat in the council chamber.

The Games included many other events, some serious, others less so. There were chariot races and boxing competitions, races with men dressed in armour, and an

event called the Pankration, a fierce and dangerous all-in fight in which only biting and gouging out the eyes were forbidden, and which the Greeks generally considered a comic turn.

Other pastimes

After exercising in the gymnasium, Greek boys had a few hours of freedom in the late afternoon in which to enjoy themselves.

Paintings on vases and sculptures often show them fishing, and also hunting. Hunting, mainly for hares, was generally done on foot, with the hares being driven into specially prepared nets. Sometimes the richer Greeks rode out after deer — riding was considered an aristocratic pastime, and only the rich could afford horses. Other scenes show boys swimming — an important skill in a land where the sea was never far away, and particularly so in Athens, a maritime state which depended on the sea both for trade and for defence.

33 Boys practising sports and games. The flat plate on the right is a discus. The man in the toga is probably a teacher.

34 Games were held in honour of the gods. Here the goddess Artemis Bendis receives the torch which had been passed from horseman to horseman in the race held in her honour.

There were a variety of ball games, the rules of which it is difficult to make out, but which seem to have resembled in some cases rugby, in others hockey. Another common if rather cruel pastime was gambling on the outcome of a cock- or quailfight.

A visit to the theatre

One of the great highlights of the year for any Greek, young or old, was a visit to the theatre. Plays were only put on for ten days each year, and were great social and religious occasions. In Athens, during the drama festivals, all business was suspended, the law courts were closed, and prisoners released from jail.

The theatres themselves were vast, semicircular, outdoor amphitheatres, with tiered seats built out of stone. The performances started at dawn and lasted all day. The audience brought food with them to eat

35 "The Jockey of Artemision". The figure has been pieced together from many fragments. The horse on which the jockey was sitting proved impossible to reconstruct in the same way.

36 Sculpture of the fifth century BC, showing what looks like an early form of hockey.

37 A tragic mask.

38 A comic mask. ➤

during the short intervals between plays.

Each play was performed only once, and a typical day's festival of plays might consist of three tragedies, a short satyr farce (with the actors wearing horses' tails and ears) and a comedy. In most cases the plots were based on well-known myths and legends, and would already be familiar to the audience. What was more interesting to the Greeks was the way the playwright treated the story and the approach he used.

The style of acting, too, was very different from our own. All the parts were played by men. The actors wore huge masks, made of stiffened linen, which they changed as the story progressed, to represent different moods. The lines were declaimed, in a loud

voice (everything had to be on a large scale
to be even comprehensible in that vast
auditorium). And there was a chorus which
acted as narrator, carrying along the thread
of the story.

At each festival a jury of citizens judged
the plays, and awarded prizes to the winners
(usually a wreath of ivy).

Play-going, which started as part of a
religious festival, was considered so important in Ancient Greece that the admission
charge was refunded to those who could not
afford it; and playgoers could even ask to
be reimbursed for the loss of a day's wages!

Growing up

An Athenian boy left school at fifteen and
was then usually apprenticed to a craftsman: an ancient law said that every boy
must learn a trade.

There was very little large-scale industry
in Greece, and most craftsmen worked in
small workshops, helped perhaps by an
apprentice and a couple of slaves. There,
depending on the type of workshop, the
boy might learn how to fire clay or decor-
ate a vase, make a shoe, sculpt a figure in
wood or stone, or cast in bronze.

In later years many of these tasks were
done by immigrants, either non-Athenian
Greeks or slaves. This gave the Athenian
citizens more time to concentrate on running
their state.

Democracy in action

Every adult male Athenian citizen took part
in the government of his city. Unlike our
representative democracies, in which one

man is elected to speak for many, Athens
was a true democracy: every man spoke
for himself. This system only worked because
Athens was both small (in terms of population) and strong (in terms of civic aware-
ness and pride).

Every year, nearly one fifth of the 40,000
Athenian citizens took their turn as judges,
public officials and council members. Each
job was held for a year. It was possible for
a man to be a general one year, and an
ordinary soldier the next. Nearly all state
jobs were part-time.

Even when he was not serving as an
official, an Athenian citizen took part in
government through the Assembly, which
was a gathering of all the citizens. It decided
such crucial matters as state expenditure,
new laws, the amount of taxes or a declara-
tion of war. It was the Assembly that elected
the state officials each year, and passed
resolutions of disapproval if they did not
agree with what the officials were doing.
All citizens were encouraged to attend the
Assembly gatherings, and to speak their
mind — which is why the Athenian craftsmen needed apprentices and slaves to help
in the workshops when they themselves
were busy with civic duties.

Further education

There were no universities in Ancient
Greece. If, having left school, a Greek
wanted to continue with his education,
he had to find his own teacher. There were

40

a number of great men, doctors, philosophers, scientists, mathematicians, who gave impromptu classes in the street, or in the corner of the market place or the gymnasium.

Socrates was one of the greatest Greek teachers and philosophers. His lessons, as described by Plato and others, took the form of questions and answers, or dialogues between himself and his students, in which Socrates asked questions and appeared naive, and all the time was pushing the student towards a better understanding of what he did not know, and of the world in general.

40 A nineteenth-century portrayal of Socrates talking to Alcibiades.

For most Greeks, however, their real education was continued in the places of assembly, and in general conversation with their fellow citizens — in the market place and gymnasium, at the theatre, during religious processions, and at intimate supper parties. For the Greeks then as now were great talkers, and nothing delighted them more than to impart the knowledge they had acquired to one however slightly less knowledgeable.

6 Girls - A Preparation for Marriage

Just as Athenian boys learned to be citizens and men, so Greek girls prepared themselves for their role in life, as housewives and mothers.

Education

Most Greek girls had little formal education. A few learned to read and write at home, under the supervision of a home tutor, but generally a respectable woman was brought up "seeing and hearing as little as possible, and asking as few questions as possible". The playwright Menander advised that "the loom is women's work, and not

debate". Another asked: "Do you know anyone with whom you have less conversation than your wife?"

However, women were not despised for their lack of education, but were admired for the skill with which they ran their households.

Household duties

The young Greek girl had plenty to learn. She had to discover the intricacies of spinning fleece into wool, and how to work the

41 Women kneading dough for bread.

weaving loom. When she married it would be her job to make all the clothes for the family.

She had to learn about cooking, and also storekeeping. Although her husband would do the actual shopping, it was part of her duties to make sure that the provisions were stored properly, so that they didn't deteriorate, and also to keep an eye on the quantities consumed, so that the household didn't suddenly run out of some vital commodity. She had to grind the wheat for bread, and stock up on supplies for the winter. A Greek wife was usually also in charge of the household finances.

She had to know a little about basic nursing, so that she could care for her husband, children or any of the slaves if they fell sick. In many cases she also had to look after her husband's parents in their old age, and sometimes her own too. She had to make sure that any visitors to the

42 A picture taken from a water pitcher, showing women fetching water from five fountain-heads.

house were made welcome, for hospitality was a sacred duty.

There was water to be fetched from the well, and the courtyard to be swept clean; younger children to be played with, domestic slaves to be supervised. In an age without any gadgets or labour-saving devices, running a house, even with the help of slaves, was a full-time occupation demanding considerable talents and ingenuity. From the age of about six, a Greek daughter was expected to help her mother wherever possible and, in so doing, to pick up the skills she was shortly going to need herself.

Going out

On the whole, respectable Greek wives rarely left their homes — except perhaps occasionally to visit a friend, or to go to the

out of sight of men. The great Athenian orator and statesman Pericles had this to say: "The best reputation a woman can have is not to be spoken of among men — either for good or for evil."

The major and often only exceptions to this staying-at-home rule were the religious festivals.

Religion

Religion played an important part in the lives of all Greeks.

They did not believe in just one god, but had a multiplicity of gods and goddesses, a whole divine family. They believed that the gods were just like men, only on a larger scale, with the same greeds, fears and jealousies as men. They also believed that each god or goddess took special care of a particular aspect of life or a particular craft, whether Hephaestus the god of fire and of blacksmiths, or Artemis the goddess of hunting. For a list of all the major Greek gods and goddesses and their characteristics, see page 66.

Each family had its own household gods, to which women would make a small daily offering at the household shrine. The Greeks were generally very superstitious, and would seek to propitiate the gods before any important undertaking.

A religious festival

Each city-state had a patron god, who was supposed to keep the city from harm. Every year the citizens would organize a great festival in honour of their patron god, or goddess. The goddess of Athens was called Athena (also goddess of wisdom), and her

theatre — and when they did, they were always accompanied by at least one servant. This was even more the case with unmarried girls past the age of puberty.

Women were expected to stay at home,

44

45

45 The Parthenon on the Acropolis — the main temple of Athena.

festival was held over three days in August.

The festival of Athena started with a relay torch race from the city walls to the Acropolis, the rocky mound in the centre of Athens on which Athens' main temple, the Parthenon, was built. The winner of the race was allowed to light the sacred fire on the altar.

The following day, at dawn, the whole city set out in procession towards the Acropolis. At the head of the procession went young girls dressed in white bearing gold cups and incense burners. They were followed by white cattle, sheep and goats, sacrificial offerings to the goddess; behind them came dancers, and musicians playing flutes. A new embroidered tunic was brought to put on Athena's statue (even goddesses had to have new clothes). Officials and priests followed, and behind them came all the rest of the citizens, decked out in their finest regalia.

After a simple ceremony the sacrificial animals were slaughtered, and the meat roasted so that Athena could enjoy the smell. Then there was a great feast, in which all the city's inhabitants took part (this was one of the few times each year that most Athenians ate meat). The feast was followed by two days of celebration, with games and poetry competitions, singing and dancing.

Women and young girls played an important part in religious ceremonies. They were

46 A reconstruction of the inside of the Parthenon, ➤ with the great statue of Athena, protectress of Athens.

46

47 A nineteenth-century artist's impression of the oracle at Delphi. The priestess went into a trance and was believed to deliver messages from Apollo. Sometimes these were very cryptic.

considered symbols of purity and goodness, and often served as handmaidens to the priests. Sometimes there were priestesses too. At the special "oracle" at Delphi, where the Greeks went for advice and guidance from the god Apollo, there was a priestess called the Pythia. In a trance, she would speak out the god's answer to men's queries.

Religious festivals and processions provided one opportunity for young girls to mingle with the rest of the population.

Betrothal and wedding

A Greek girl's husband was chosen for her by her father, who also had to provide his daughter with a considerable dowry. Girls usually married young, at about fourteen or fifteen, though their husbands were generally much older, perhaps thirty or even thirty-five.

The long and complicated marriage ceremonies were designed to ease the transfer of the bride from one household to the other, and to ensure the fertility and prosperity of the new household.

As a first step, on the eve of her wedding day, the bride had to renounce her playthings, and, symbolically, all her youthful pleasures. Her dolls, along with other gifts and a lock of her hair, were dedicated to the goddess Artemis. She then took a special bridal bath. The water for this was fetched in procession by all the women of the household carrying tall pottery jars and accompanied by a flute-player.

The wedding ceremony

On the wedding day itself the house of the

bride's parents was decorated with garlands of flowers. A sacrifice was made to the gods, and this was followed by a grand banquet for all members of the bride's family, her friends and relatives. The bride wore a veil, and was attended by an older woman who advised her and showed her what to do at each stage of the ceremony. The bridegroom also came to the banquet, with an attendant or best man. As well as the sacrificial meat, there was a special wedding cake (or cakes), flavoured with sesame seed, which was believed to encourage fertility.

In the evening the bride gathered together a few symbolic household objects, perhaps a knife and a jar, before leaving the security of her family home. She then climbed into a cart with the groom, and the best man drove them to the bridegroom's home. The rest of her family and wedding guests followed behind in procession, with torches, flutes and songs.

48 Men, women and children bring offerings to Artemis, goddess of hunting (notice the sacred deer), and protectress of virgins and young girls.

On arrival the bride was formally welcomed into her new household by the bridegroom's parents. A procession was formed, and the bridegroom led her by hand to the household shrine while grain and fruit were showered on them, before taking her off to the marriage chamber.

The following day there were further celebrations; the wedding guests brought presents, and there was music and dancing.

A wedding provided one of the few occasions in Ancient Greece when whole families, men and women and children, dined and danced together, and so was a high point in family life.

Married life
As we have seen, Greek men spent very little time at home. Even the evening meal, the main meal of the day, was usually taken in company just with men (or, if not just men, then certainly not with wives). At the same time, this has to be reconciled with the large number of simple domestic scenes depicted on pottery and in paintings, and the undoubted affection and strong bond of

companionship between man and wife reflected in Greek plays and poetry.

Perhaps it had something to do with the division of labour; the fact that the wife, though she had few rights outside the home, inside the home was all-powerful and much to be respected; and that, when husband and wife did see each other, they had nothing to discuss or worry about, but could get on with enjoying each other's company.

49 A warrior about to leave home. Many pictures reveal an affectionate relationship between man and wife.

7 Spartan Discipline

So far this book has been mainly about Athens, partly because more is known about it, and partly because the way things were done in Athens was typical, to a greater or lesser extent, of the rest of Greece. One city-state, however, stands out from this: the military state of Sparta.

Sparta's history
At the end of the Mycenaean age, in about 1200 BC, warlike tribes from the north overran most of Greece. One particular tribe, the Dorians, invaded the southern part of the Peloponnese, conquering the region known as Laconia. Unlike the invaders in the rest of Greece, the Dorians (or Spartans, as they became known, after their chief city Sparta) did not mingle with the existing population of the area. Instead, they enslaved the original inhabitants, gave them the name of Helots, and set them to work the land for them. Meanwhile the Dorians established a large and well-trained army to keep control.

Spartan society
Spartan society was arranged in a totally different way from the rest of Greece. At the top were the town-dwelling Spartan citizens, descendants of the Dorian invaders. Below them there was a free class living in small villages, but with no political or voting rights; they were known as "neighbours", or Perioikoi. And at the bottom were the Helots, or agricultural slaves. The Helots were not the slaves of individual Spartan citizens, but of the whole Spartan community. They worked on the land, under the supervision of Spartans, and had to contribute half the produce to the citizen whose land it was.

With a large labour force to provide the essential food, the Spartan citizens were freed from the necessity of tilling the land. At the same time, with such a large slave population (many times the size of the citizen body), the Spartan state was forced to organize itself along military lines in order to keep control, and to put down the sporadic Helot uprisings.

We might imagine that the Spartan citizen, with Helots to do all the work for him, would lead a life of idleness and luxury. In fact, it is probably true to say that the life of the average Spartan citizen was considerably harsher and more uncomfortable than that of any Helot. This was partly the result of the Spartans' feeling that they were unique, separate, different from anybody else, so that they had higher expectations of themselves. In straining for individual excellence they pushed themselves, and particularly their bodies, to the very limits of endurance. Then, the need for a large standing army to keep the Helot population under control meant that the state had to be organized along military lines, with almost every adult male a full-time member of the fighting team. In time, as the number of Spartan citizens diminished, and the Helot population grew, the pressure on the army, and so on all Spartan citizens, became greater and greater. Gradually, interest in the arts declined, all charm and grace disappeared from Spartan life, and by the Classical period the whole state was organized into one giant military machine.

Yet, despite the unprepossessing and rather grim aspects of Spartan society, there were many Greeks in the Classical period who admired the Spartan ideal: the pursuit of excellence by means of rigorous discipline and self-denial. It is certainly something we have rather lost sight of in the modern world.

Growing up in Sparta

Unlike in other Greek states, when a Spartan child was born the decision whether or not to abandon it lay not with the father but with the state. In considering whether the child should live or not, the state was deciding whether the child was strong enough to contribute fully to the military machine. The emphasis was entirely on physical prowess, a strong body, straight limbs, a healthy bawl, rather than on any considerations of beauty or parental love.

If the child was allowed to live, he spent the first six years with his mother, as was usual in Greece. But unlike other Greek children, with their cosseted early years, the Spartan child was encouraged from the very first to be tough and warrior-like. Not for him the carefree childhood and loving family life found in other cities. All the games he was allowed to play were structured to develop strong muscles and self-discipline, the ability to endure pain and discomfort.

At the age of seven the Spartan boy was removed from his mother, and entered into a period of strict training, which lasted until he was about twenty. Usually he was attached to a "pack", a gang of some twenty or so youths under the leadership of an older boy.

Schooling as such, learning to read and to write, was minimal. The main emphasis was always on discipline and exercise. Generally, children were made to go about barefoot and without any clothes, to accustom them to hardship and discomfort and to toughen their powers of endurance. Fighting was encouraged, provided it was not in anger. Those fighting had to stop the minute they were ordered to do so. Complete obedience was essential.

The food allowance for children was strictly rationed, and the food was always designed for nourishment, to keep body and soul together, rather than for enjoyment. Spartan children's diet was also kept to a minimum, strange as it may seem to us now, in order to encourage them to steal. It was believed that, in this way, children would learn how to live off the land. And since they were stealing from the Helots, rather than from Spartan citizens, there was no disgrace involved. The children who were caught stealing were punished, but the punishment was for being caught, not for the fact of stealing.

The boy and the fox

Spartan morals were very different from our own, and the ideals the Spartans looked up to sometimes seem strange to us. A famous Spartan moral tale tells the story of a young boy, out with a thieving party, who stole a fox and hid it under his cloak. Back at the camp the fox began to gnaw at the boy's stomach. The boy realized that to set the fox free would mean discovery and therefore disgrace. So he said nothing, did nothing, and allowed the fox to continue gnawing away. Eventually the boy dropped down dead, his stomach in shreds but his honour intact.

The "pack"

At roughly the age of fourteen Spartan boys began their military training. The discipline was stepped up and the punishments became even harsher. There were periods of complete retreat, when the young Spartan had to survive on his own in the mountains, living off the land, finding his own food and water, and building his own shelter. And there were ordeals of great severity, including a whipping ceremony which later became a tourist attraction for visiting Romans. The boys lived in communal messes, and had no private possessions of their own. Every aspect of their life was open to discussion and criticism; nothing was considered private in the "pack".

The idea behind this was to build Spartan youth into a cohesive fighting force, one whose bodies could be pushed beyond the normal limits, who could endure hunger, thirst and extremes of temperature, who would not flinch from pain or danger and did not easily tire. At the same time, because the members of a "pack" endured so many hardships together, they developed a strong sense of unity as a fighting force. And because they were able to endure more than the average, they had high expectations of themselves, and a strong sense of moral superiority. Cowardice was the greatest disgrace. When saying goodbye to her son before he went off to battle, a Spartan mother would say that he must return either carrying his shield or lying on it (the traditional way to bring home the dead). To lose one's shield was a sign of cowardice, of having run away from the enemy, and even a mother would prefer her son dead to that disgrace.

Spartan virtues

But the Spartan picture is not one of unredeemed harshness. Although other Greeks joked about the Spartans, their rigid ways, their often inhuman values, they admired them too, for the other side of that coin. The Spartans had an ideal, a very exacting one, one which gave meaning to their lives and could make them justifiably proud of being Spartan. And in trying to live up to that ideal, they often put into practice virtues that others only preached.

The Roman historian Plutarch recorded

this story, for example. At the Olympic Games one year, an old man was stumbling to and fro looking for a seat. As he passed by Corinthians, Athenians and others crowded there, he was ignored or jeered at. He came at last, however, to where the Spartans sat, and immediately every young man and many older ones too leapt up to offer him their seat. Seeing this the crowd clapped, applauding the Spartan example. And the old man sighed to himself, saying: "All Greeks *know* what is right, but only the Spartans *do* it."

Spartan girls

The upbringing of Spartan girls was not quite as harsh as that of their brothers, but it was certainly considerably more strenuous than that of Greek girls in other states. A Spartan girl was expected to do hard physical training so that she would bear strong and healthy children. Girls competed with boys in athletics and other events, sometimes wearing so little that even the imperturbable Greeks were shocked.

Life in the Spartan army

At the age of twenty a Spartan youth underwent a series of difficult initiation tests before being admitted into the army. But even though now considered an adult and a citizen, the Spartan was still in the grip of the state system. He continued to live in large barracks, sleeping in dormitories and eating in communal messes known as *phiditia*. Only after the age of thirty was a Spartan allowed to sleep at home.

Each Spartan soldier had to contribute a fixed amount of provisions to his mess: barley, wine, cheese, fruit and meat. These provisions came from his farm, the land allotted to him by the state and which was worked for him by Helots. If he failed to contribute his share, he ceased for a time to be considered a full citizen. The Spartan himself, however, was forbidden to engage in agriculture or in trade. He had to be a soldier.

50 A reconstruction of the Dromos (race-course) in Sparta.

This communal life for the Spartan soldier did not change even when he got married. In the Spartan marriage ceremony, the bride had her hair cut short and wore male clothing. After the wedding the husband was only allowed to visit his wife in secret, and had to return to sleep in the dormitory.

The Spartan soldier spent two years of his army life as part of the secret police, whose task it was to hunt down and kill any troublesome Helots. The constant fear of Helot uprising was the main reason why the Spartan state was organized along such military lines: they were a very small citizen-body holding down a much larger slave population.

Everything a Spartan did was open to criticism by his peers; and if a Spartan was considered to have acted disgracefully, harsh punishments were imposed, or he was ostracized by his companions.

The hoplite system

The military training of the Spartans, their emphasis on corporate spirit and immense self-discipline, was designed to produce a particular type of soldier: not the brave and reckless individual warriors described in Homer's epics, but the steadfast, disciplined soldiers of the line, or "phalanx", which came into prominence in Greece after the eighth century BC.

The phalanx was a long block of soldiers several ranks deep, organized in files from front to back. As one man in a file fell, his place would be taken by the man behind. In an army organized in phalanxes, the most important virtue was steadfastness — steadiness in charging together, or in standing still against an onslaught.

The new type of warriors were called hoplites (or armoured men). They wore a bronze helmet, bronze greaves to protect their legs, and a cuirass made out of either bronze or, later, linen, to protect their chests. They were armed with a short

51 The monument to Leonidas and his Spartan defenders at Thermopylae (see page 14).

sword, and a long-reaching spear for thrusting. In addition, Spartan hoplites wore a scarlet cloak, which became the symbol of Spartan militarism.

Other Greek states also had hoplite armies, but the Spartan army was acknowledged throughout Greece as the best. Few states would choose to fight a set battle against the Spartans.

A Spartan citizen

At the age of thirty a Spartan man was allowed to leave his mess and go to live at home. But even here he was not free of the army. He was not allowed to take part in agriculture (this was all done by the Helots who tilled his land for him); he was discouraged from entering into trade. Indeed, to stop people from trying to amass a fortune, the Spartans abolished the gold currency prevalent elsewhere in Greece, and instead had a clumsy currency based on bars of iron — you needed to collect an immense number of these in order to have any fortune at all!

Every Spartan citizen was liable to instant call-up into the army. The call-up was done by age groups, starting with the youngest. Veterans were only called up in a real emergency, when they would look after the baggage train, and the wounded.

Once he had left the army, the Spartan citizen was supposed to devote his life to

52 A Spartan warrior. Only the rich could afford horses. More typically, Spartan warriors were infantrymen.

passing on what he had learned: lecturing to young soldiers, supervising their training, making sure they maintained a high standard of discipline, punishing those who failed, leading the army into battle, and, of course, producing strong children to form the next generation of hoplites.

Spartan democracy

Although it was in a sense a democracy, the Spartan constitution was very complicated. There were two elected "kings" (two so that no one would have overall control); in battle the army was commanded by one of the kings. As in other Greek cities, there was an Assembly at which every Spartan citizen was entitled to vote. The voting, however, was done by shouting. The group who shouted the loudest won the day!

8 Work and Workers

Apart from Spartans, most Greek boys, when they grew up, had to do something to earn a living. Learning and practising a trade, entering into commerce, or looking after the estate were the most common ways for the better-off citizens to employ their time. They often had slaves to do the actual work.

Work on the land

It may seem that most Greeks were city-dwellers, and that, like city-dwellers today, they had little contact with the land. In fact, however, agriculture and land-ownership formed the basis and yardstick of Greek society.

Towns were small, and countryside and fields were never far away. Most Greeks either lived in the town and travelled out every morning to till their fields; or lived on their farms and came daily into the city to play their part in its Assembly and law-courts. Town and country were inextricably linked.

53 Earliest agriculture in Greece.

Even the smallest landowner usually had at least one or two slaves to help him in his work; and at harvest time all able bodies would be roped in to help.

The soil in Greece is poor; much of the countryside is barren mountain or very rocky, and farming in ancient times, with primitive tools, was very hard work. The main crops in the plains were barley or wheat, and also olives, figs and vines.

The wealth of Athens was based on her olive groves and the export of olive oil. But olive groves take a long time to grow (an olive tree needs some sixteen years to become properly established and bear fruit), and this made them particularly vulnerable to attack by raiding parties during inter-city squabbles.

54 Detail from an *amphora,* showing a man sowing. The seed is sown "broadcast".

Farming methods

Decorations on Greek vases and pottery show mules yoked together, and oxen ploughing a field; seed being sown "broadcast", that is, being scattered by hand into the furrows; harvesting wheat, and then threshing it to separate the grain; tending vines; shaking down olives from the olive trees; and taking the farm produce to market.

Livestock were kept: a couple of oxen for ploughing, sheep and goats for milk and fleece, and perhaps some pigs as well. Bee-keeping was also common, as honey was the only form of sweetening (it is still much used in Greek recipes today).

55 Taking the farm produce to market.

Greek agriculture was fairly primitive. They did not know how to keep land fertile by rotating crops, and instead used to leave their fields fallow every second year to replenish the soil. Their farming implements were extremely crude and probably not very effective on the hard ground. This, combined with the poverty of the soil itself, meant that most Greek city-states were not self-sufficient in food, and had to import wheat in particular, usually from Egypt or the rich lands of the Caucasus (part of modern Russia).

This lack of self-sufficiency in food periodically forced the Greeks to send out colonization parties to settle in other countries, as a way of easing pressure on the land available, and also to take sometimes extreme measures to limit the population. At the same time what the Greeks did produce

61

was renowned for its excellent quality, and played an important role in the "balance of payments". In particular, wine, olive oil and wool were staple exports and were traded all over the Mediterranean.

Life for a Greek farmer, then, could be hard work and worrying, particularly in a hot summer, or when a raiding party was about; but could also be extremely profitable.

Craftsmen

After agriculture, the most common Greek occupation was that of craftsman. There were many different sorts of craftsmen: potters, metalworkers, stone masons, sculptors, carpenters, cobblers.

Although between them they produced many goods for sale, often following a similar pattern, there was no large-scale production or factories of any sort. Each craftsman was his own master, working in his own small workshop, with the help of a few slaves and perhaps an apprentice.

Even the building of something like the Parthenon in Athens, for example, although a colossal undertaking, was done by hundreds and thousands of individual craftsmen, each tendering for and being paid for one small item of work. In such cases the craftsman would usually leave his workshop and work on site for the duration of the contract.

Craftsmen working on a public building of this kind were paid a standard daily rate of one drachma, whether they were the architect, the stone mason or the builder's labourer. There were no variations according to skill.

Like the farmer, the craftsman would usually leave his work in charge of slaves in the afternoon so that he could go to take part in the governing of his city.

The Greek who wanted to buy a vase, or a pair of shoes, some jewellery or a statuette to go in his household shrine would visit the

56 Casting bronze.

62

craftsman's shop and order what he wanted. One of the busiest of Greek craftsmen was the potter, since almost all household goods, from lamps and cooking pots to tiles and toys, were made of clay. The black glaze and fine design found on Athenian pots was admired all over the ancient world, and Athens exported pottery throughout the Mediterranean.

Trade

Trade in the ancient world was a business of high risks and high profits. Ships set out from Greek ports laden with goods for sale: olive oil in tall jars known as *amphorae* (the remains of which can be found in many

57 A shoe-maker's shop.

countries around the Mediterranean), the tasty black olives themselves, wine, and fine woollen cloth, pottery and silver.

All these goods had to be paid for by the trader before he started on his journey, and yet he could never be sure of his market. He would have to run the risk of storms at sea, of pirates, of a war breaking out; the risk of capture and being enslaved, or of travelling to unknown lands where he and his goods might not be welcome. Then, having sold what he took with him, he would undertake to buy other things for the return journey: unusual items which took

58 An *amphora,* used for storing olive oil.

his fancy, and which he thought the citizens back home would snap up in the market place; or staple commodities, such as wheat, if he could find them, which he knew were always lacking and therefore would be welcome. The round trip might take up to a year or more, a year of danger and discomfort. If the journey was successful, the profits were enormous. But many journeys were not successful.

Many of the most prosperous Greek traders and merchants were not proper citizens, but "metics" or foreigners, who had settled in a city and made their home there, but were not accorded full rights of citizenship or a vote in the way the city was run.

Slaves

Throughout this book slaves have been shadowy figures in the background, with their existence taken very much for granted. That is because that is the way the Ancient Greeks thought of them. For the Greeks, the existence of slavery was one of the facts of life.

It may seem strange to us that the Ancient Greeks, champions of democracy and freedom and individual liberty, should have allowed to persist in their midst a system which appeared so fundamentally to deny everything they stood for. But the Greeks themselves did not see it that way. For them, slavery was something that could happen to anyone; they did not despise or look down on their slaves; they treated them fairly, on the whole, and kindly;

but they used them, since that was the way of the world.

The children of slaves, or children captured and enslaved, were looked after well and taught a trade or craft. This might be helping on the farm or in the workshop, working in the home as a household slave, serving on board ship in the navy, or doing any other tasks that the master thought the slave showed aptitude for.

Girl slaves either worked in the house as handmaidens, cleaning and sewing, fetching water, looking after the children; or else were trained as dancing girls, to entertain men at their dinner parties. They were taught to play the lyre, to sing and to dance. As can be imagined, the prettier ones were much in demand.

Slaves practising a craft were paid for the work they did, and handed over either all or most of what they earned to their masters in return for their keep. In this way a master could actually make a profit out of slave-owning. But slaves were also usually allowed to keep a proportion of their earnings, and to spend the money however they liked. Some bought themselves fine clothes, so that bemused citizens would sometimes say that slaves were better dressed than any citizen. Others saved up the money and sometimes managed to buy their freedom.

Slaves could be and were released, by buying their own freedom, or by having their ransom paid by friends or relatives from their home state. Other slaves were released by their masters as a token of gratitude for long service, or as a gift in their will. Masters and slaves often became close friends, as is attested by numerous tombstone inscriptions.

The only flaw in this otherwise rather rosy picture of slavery in Ancient Greece is the case of the slaves working in the silver mines at Laurium near Athens. Here thousands of slaves, chosen from each newly arrived batch in the market place for their brutish looks, physical strength, and seeming lack of intelligence, were sent to work in dark, cramped and dangerous conditions underground, mining out the silver that helped to make Athens so prosperous. Their life expectancy was very short, not more than a few months in many cases, and they seem to have been very harshly treated. For them it was the whip rather than kind words and fine clothes. And so we are left, once again, with the rather uncomfortable feeling that the Ancient Greeks, so admirable in so many ways, chose to turn their backs on and ignore this one rather ignoble aspect of their own society.

Gods and Goddesses

There were thousands of Greek gods and goddesses. Each looked after a particular aspect of life, a particular craft or community. Although the Greeks believed that their gods had superhuman powers, they also believed that they were subject to many of the same fears, jealousies and joys as humans, and that these emotions caused repercussions on earth. Most of the gods were related in one large family, and their home was believed to be on Mount Olympus.

Aphrodite	the goddess of love, and the most beautiful of the goddesses. She protected lovers.
Apollo	the son of Zeus, he was the god of light, and also of music and healing. Each day he rode his chariot across the sky and ushered in the day.
Artemis	twin-sister of Apollo, she spent her time hunting. Her arrows brought sudden death. She protected virgins and young girls.
Asclepius	son of Apollo and god of healing. He was struck dead for defying the laws of nature.
Athena	the daughter of Zeus and the goddess of wisdom. She was believed to have invented the potter's wheel, and to protect all craftsmen. She was also the special goddess and protector of the city of Athens.
Demeter	the goddess of corn, and of the fruitful earth. The Greeks believed that each year her daughter Persephone spent six months with Hades in the underworld, and that it was Demeter's sorrow over this which caused the winter.
Dionysos	the god of wine. The Greek drama festivals were held in his honour.
Hades	the brother of Zeus and the god of the underworld.
Hephaestus	son of Zeus, he taught men how to use fire to work metals, and was the protector of blacksmiths.
Hera	the third wife of Zeus (the other two were Maia and Themis). She protected wives and mothers.
Hermes	the messenger of the gods, and also inventor of the lyre. He protected traders and travellers, and led the dead to the underworld.
Hestia	Zeus's older sister, and goddess of the household hearth. She protected homes and families, and also the city.
Pan	the god of woods and pastures, and protector of shepherds and their flocks. He was believed to have a goat's horns, ears and legs.
Poseidon	brother and one-time rival of Zeus, he was the god of the sea. He caused earthquakes and storms, and was especially feared by sailors.
Themis	the second wife of Zeus, and goddess of justice. In her scales she weighed the innocent and the guilty.
Zeus	the father of the gods, and ruler of Olympus. Thunder was believed to be his voice. He was the protector of all Greece, and the Olympic Games were held in his honour.

Date List

BC

c. 1600-1200	Mycenaean age
	Period described by Homer in his epic poems
1200	Traditional date for the siege of Troy
c. 1150-950	Dark Ages, and a series of invasions
c. 950	Beginning of the Archaic period, and a revival of Greek culture and civilization
c. 850	Traditional date of Homer
776	Traditional date of first Olympic Games
c. 735	Start of Greek colonization of Sicily and southern Italy
c. 650	Tyrannies set up, and overthrown, all over Greece
594	Solon appointed chief magistrate (*archon*) of Athens; introduces democracy and codifies laws
490	Athenians defeat Persian army at Marathon
480	Persian Emperor Xerxes launches large force against the Greeks and is defeated by Spartans at Thermopylae
	Persian navy routed by Athenians at Salamis
472	First surviving play by Aeschylus
468	Sophocles wins tragedy prize
459-454	First Peloponnesian War between Athens and Sparta
455	First play by Euripides
	Birth of Thucydides
447	Work begun on the Parthenon
431	War again between Athens and Sparta
429	Death of Pericles
	Birth of Plato
427	First play by Aristophanes
411-410	Revolution of "Four Hundred" at Athens
	Oligarchy established
404	Athens surrenders to Sparta
399	Trial and execution of Socrates at Athens
359	Accession of Philip II of Macedon
	Greece united
336	Philip II succeeded by Alexander ("the Great")
334	Alexander invades Asia
c. 300-146	Hellenistic age
	Alexandria takes over from Athens as centre of learning
146	Greece becomes part of Roman Empire

Glossary

acropolis	a fortress on a hill around which towns grew up
agora	market place; the central area in a Greek city where the citizens met to discuss their business
amphora	tall pottery jar, used in particular to store olive oil (plural *amphorae*)
archon	a Greek official elected by the citizens
arete	excelling in all aspects of life, both intellectual and physical; this was the goal of many Greeks
chiton	a tunic, made out of one piece of cloth
democracy	(rule by the people) a form of government where the state is ruled by all the citizens, and officials are regularly elected
discus	a flat and circular bronze plate thrown in athletic competitions
Dorians	warlike people who invaded Greece in the twelfth century BC; the Spartans were Dorians
gymnasium	an exercise ground; also used for holding open-air classes
Helots	slaves used by the Spartans to run their farms
hoplites	heavily armoured soldiers
javelin	a long spear, about the height of a man
krater	a large vase used for mixing wine and water
metics	foreigners who had settled in a city and were allowed to work there, but had no citizenship rights
Mycenaean	of Mycenae; used to describe the Bronze Age civilization that flourished in Greece from about 1600 to 1200 BC; the word derives from the name of the citadel where remains of the civilization were first discovered
oligarchy	(rule by a few) a system of government where the state is ruled by a small group of people
paedagogus	literally a "boy-leader"; an elderly slave whose job was to accompany a young boy to school, and to supervise his moral development.
palaestra	a training ground for athletes
Pankration	an all-in fight, with no holds barred; one of the events of the ancient Olympic Games
papyrus	paper; this was usually imported from Egypt, and was very expensive
Pentathlon	the most famous event of the Olympic Games, consisting of five separate contests: running, discus throwing, long jump, wrestling and javelin throwing
Perioikoi	literally "dwellers around"; villagers who lived around Sparta, who were not enslaved like the Helots, but were not citizens of Sparta either
phalanx	military formation of soldiers arranged in a block of files
phiditia	communal messes used by Spartan soldiers

polis	originally meant the same as acropolis; later came to be used to mean the whole city-state
Pythia	the priestess of the oracle at Delphi who, in her trances, was believed to foretell the future
rhetoric	the art of speaking in public, and of convincing argument
strigil	an instrument with a smooth curved blade used by the Greeks to scrape and clean the skin
stylus	an instrument with a sharp point at one end used for writing on wax coated tablets; the other end of the stylus was flat and was used to wipe the tablet clean
symposium	an organized drinking party
tyrannus	a single strong ruler; hence "tyranny", the third form of government common in Ancient Greece

Books for Further Reading

All the books listed here should be easily obtainable.

Connolly, Peter, *The Greek Armies*, Macdonald Educational, 1977. The story of Greek arms and armour, and military exploits, from the siege of Troy to Alexander the Great.

Crosher, Judith, *The Greeks*, Macdonald Educational, 1974. A look at everyday life in Ancient Greece, with numerous full-colour illustrations.

Taylor, Duncan, *Ancient Greece*, Methuen Outlines, 1957. Good introduction to the history of Ancient Greece.

Life in Ancient Greece — Pictures from Pottery, Longman Young Books, 1973. An unusual look at the Ancient Greeks, based entirely on scenes depicted on their pottery.

More difficult

Andrewes, Antony, *Greek Society*, Pelican, 1971. A sound and comprehensive study.

Kitto, H.D.F., *The Greeks*, Penguin, 1951. Witty and lively introduction to Greek history and character.

Zimmern, Alfred, *The Greek Commonwealth*, Oxford University Press, 1971. A classic, first published in 1911, with many interesting sidelights on Greek society.

Greek authors

What the Ancient Greeks themselves wrote can also teach us a great deal about them. Look out in particular for some of the dialogues of **Plato** (*Symposium*, *Protagoras*), the plays of **Aristophanes,** and the writings of **Xenophon.** All of these are available in a number of translations.

Index

The numbers in **bold type** refer to the figure numbers of the illustrations